What Is a Fungus?

What Is a Fungus?

D. M. Souza

Franklin Watts
A Division of Scholastic Inc.
New York • Toronto • London • Auckland • Sydney
Mexico City • New Delhi • Hong Kong
Danbury, Connecticut

Note to readers: Definitions for words in **bold** can be found in the Glossary at the back of this book.

Photographs ©: Animals Animals/Michael Fogden/OSF: 38; Dembinsky Photo Assoc.: 40 (Sharon Cummings), 30 (E. R. Degginger), 32 (Rod Planck), 14 (Alex Rakosy); Dwight R. Kuhn Photography: 24, 37 bottom; Earth Scenes/Michael Fogden: 39; Peter Arnold Inc./Walter H. Hodge: 12; Photo Researchers, NY: 46 (John Bova), 37 top (Alan & Linda Detrick), 2, 45 (Gregory G. Dimijian), 44 (Don W. Fawcett), 43 (Georg Gerster), 29 (Holt Studios, Intl.), 18,19 (Jeff Lepore), 5 left, 51 (MG3/Vision), cover (Microfield Scientific, Ltd/SPL), 36 (SPL), 21 (Kenneth H. Thomas); PhotoEdit: 6 (Bill Aron), 34 (Myrleen Ferguson); Visuals Unlimited: 26 (R. Calentine), 48 (Christine Case), 31 (David Cavagnaro), 9 (J. Michael Eichelberger), 22, 23 (David M. Phillips), 20 (Dick Poe), 17 inset (G. Shih/R. Kessel), 5 right, 17 (Richard Walters).

The photograph on the cover shows a close-up of bread mold. The photograph opposite the title page shows a stinkhorn fungus in northeastern Peru.

Library of Congress Cataloging-in-Publication Data

Souza, D. M. (Dorothy M.)
    What is a fungus? / D.M. Souza.
        p. cm. — (Watts library)
    Includes bibliographical references (p.).
    ISBN 0-531-11979-3 (lib. bdg.)   0-531-16223-0 (pbk.)
    1. Fungi—Juvenile literature. [1. Fungi.] I. Title. II. Series.
QK603.5 .S68 2002
579.5—dc21   2001017565

Contents

Fungi leave a telltale trail of fuzz as they feast on bread.

Chapter One

Eating Everywhere

Open a window or a door, and thousands float inside. They are too small for the human eye to see. Some, in their search for food, land on a loaf of bread, an orange, or an open jar of jam. Others slip into a bedroom, bathtub, or closet and begin making a meal out of sweaty socks, leather shoes, shower curtains, or paper. The invaders leave a trail of white, black, green, or pink fuzz wherever they are feasting.

Secret Agent

During the American Revolution (1775–83), the wooden warships of the British had more damage done to them by hungry fungi than by the colonists' cannons.

Outside, millions are snacking on trees, flowers, insects, and small animals. Some settle on decks, front steps, porches, fences, and telephone poles and feed until these structures collapse. Others help plants and trees grow, provide food for thousands of creatures, and act as nature's super-recyclers. They can cure and poison, save and destroy, soothe and terrify.

Who are these double agents with weird appetites? They are **fungi**. (The singular term is **fungus**.) Without them, Earth would be a very different planet.

Fungi have been dining around Earth for about 400 million years. Soon after plants appeared on land, fungi probably nourished themselves on roots, leaves, and stems. When animals and humans arrived, they quickly found new sources of food and, in time, became useful to a host of creatures.

A Separate Kingdom

For hundreds of years, fungi were thought to be plants, but scientists slowly began to detect three main differences. First, unlike plants, fungi have no leaves or flowers and do not use the energy of the Sun to make their own food. Instead, they

Ancient Fungi

In 1991, hikers in the Italian Alps discovered the well-preserved remains of a man estimated to have lived more than five thousand years ago. In the man's backpack were a string of dried fungi—the kind used to start campfires—and several mushrooms that might have served as medicines.

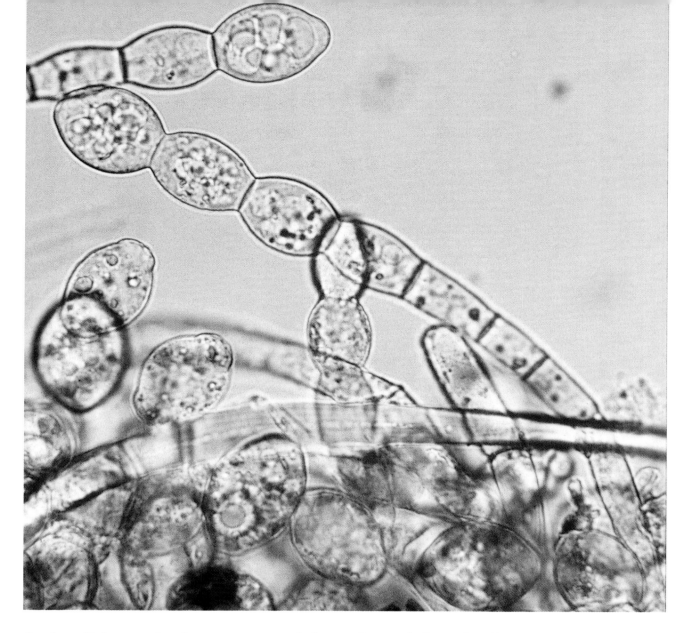

feed on living or dead matter around them. Second, fungal cell walls are made of **chitin**, a tough material found not in plants but in the outer skeleton of insects. Third, most plants reproduce by means of seeds, but fungi multiply in different ways.

Eventually fungi were placed in a kingdom, or large group,

Fungal cell walls contain chitin, a material not found in plant cells.

of their own. To date, about 200,000 different kinds of fungi have been identified. **Mycologists**, scientists who study these amazing life forms, believe millions more are waiting to be discovered.

Most fungi live in dark, moist places, but others can survive where temperatures dip below freezing or rise to 120° F (50° C). When food is scarce or the weather turns harsh, many fungi become **dormant**. As soon as conditions improve, they revive and begin growing again. They can do this even after months or years of appearing to be dead.

Classifying and Naming

After a new fungus is discovered, its structure and method of reproduction are carefully studied. Then it is placed in the series of five categories used to classify all organisms: **phylum** (plural **phyla**), class, order, family, and genus. Phylum is the largest category. Each successive group contains a smaller number of closely related fungi until only one **species**, or kind, is identified. The chart on the next page shows the classification for humans and button mushrooms, a common fungus sold in supermarkets.

Classification

Category	Humans	Button Mushrooms
Kingdom:	Animalia	Fungi
Phylum:	Chordata	Basidiomycota
Class:	Mammalia	Holobasidiomycetes
Order:	Primate	Agaricales
Family:	Hominidae	Agaricaceae
Genus:	*Homo*	*Agaricus*
Species:	*sapiens*	*bisporus*

Each fungus, like every other living thing, has a **binomial**, or two-part name, that identifies its genus and species. For example, the binomial for button mushrooms is *Agaricus bisporus*, and the one for humans is *Homo sapiens*. Binomials are always in Latin or Greek. Scientists around the world recognize and use these names no matter what language they speak.

Many fungi also have popular names that spring up around the mushrooms they produce. Names such as "witches' butter," "jack-o-lantern," and "dead man's fingers" often reflect people's fears or superstitions. For example, when a circle of mushrooms suddenly appeared overnight, some people decided it marked the spot where elves had danced the night

According to legend, fairy rings mark the spot where elves danced at night.

before. The mushrooms' caps were supposedly the seats where the elves had rested between dances. "Fairy rings" became the name for these circles, formed by the fungus *Marasmius oreades*. This and other popular names are still in use today.

Where Do They Belong?

Scientists do not always agree on how to classify fungi. Slime molds and water molds, once considered fungi, are now grouped with other living things. **Lichens** are no longer a separate phylum of fungi because they represent not a single

Four Major Phyla of Fungi

Phylum	Sample Members
Zygomycota	Bread molds, dung fungi
Ascomycota	Yeasts, powdery mildews, truffles
Chytridiomycota	Parasites of insect larvae, aquatic fungi
Basidiomycota	Mushrooms, rusts, smuts, puffballs

organism but a partnership between a fungus and an alga. Sometimes scientists uncover new organisms that look a lot like fungi but later reveal their differences. These are temporarily put in a category with other organisms until they can be carefully classified.

Mycology is a challenging study. New fungi are being discovered nearly every day. As sophisticated technologies are developed, scientists will gain a clearer understanding of each fungus, where it belongs in its kingdom, and its unique impact on the organisms surrounding it.

These spores, shown at 120 times their actual size, are forming hyphae.

Chapter Two

Growing and Reproducing

Most fungi begin their lives as **spores**. These are objects so tiny that more than 4,500 could be lined up on a piece of thread 1 inch (2.5 centimeters) long. When sprinkled with moisture, spores swell like seeds and begin growing.

Imagine one of these specks floating through an open window and landing on a moist piece of bread left on a counter-top. The spore has no mouth or teeth to help it eat. Instead, it begins to grow as a thin tube called a **hypha** (plural **hyphae**).

From its tip ooze powerful **enzymes** that slowly digest the bread. Unlike humans, fungi digest their food outside of their bodies and then absorb the nutrients that are released.

The hypha forks, then forks again, growing in different directions as it encounters more food. Each branching thread is a thousand times finer than a human hair. In a few days, the threads are twisting, turning, crisscrossing, and doubling back on themselves until they look like a mass of cobwebs. The feeding body is now called a **mycelium** (plural **mycelia**). Large mycelia can grow an astonishing 0.5 mile (0.8 kilometer) each day, but the only visible evidence is a little white fuzz on a piece of bread.

The mycelia of some molds grow very quickly. Within days, they can spread over loaves of bread, pieces of rotting fruit, or a bowl of spaghetti that has been left too long in a refrigerator. The mycelia of bread molds develop balloonlike containers at the ends of their threads. Each container is filled with new spores that ripen, fall, land on food, and begin the process of feeding and growing.

Visible Fruit

Some mycelia spread slowly but continue branching and growing for years. In 1992, a giant fungus was found underground in a Michigan forest. It covered approximately 35 acres (15 hectares) and was estimated to weigh as much as a blue whale. After fifteen hundred years, the fungus was still feasting on the roots and stumps of surrounding trees.

As the giant grew, lumps developed along its threads. From time to time, these swellings pushed upward and appeared above ground in the form of umbrella-shaped caps. Scientists found that each cap was a mushroom, a type of **fruiting body**, belonging to the same underground fungus.

Many fungi produce fruiting bodies that can push their way above ground with tremendous pressure. Mushrooms have been known to crack cement patios, lift basement floors, and move large stone slabs. Beneath the caps of some mushrooms are hundreds of pink, tissue-thin dividers, called **gills** because they look like fish gills. Lining the gills are millions of spores that either fall to the ground or are carried to new places.

Tissue-thin gills on the underside of a mushroom (Inset) A close-up of the tiny spores that line gills

Edible Mushrooms

People around the world collect mushrooms as a source of food and income. In parts of Europe, families often spend weekends searching through fields and forests for these delicacies. In North America, fans of fungi form mushroom clubs whose members trek through the woods hunting for edible wild mushrooms. The Morel Mushroom Hunting Club, based in Alachua, Florida, provides services and information to morel, chanterelle, bolete, and oyster mushroom hunters. Its members come from the United States, Canada, and several other countries.

Bird's nest fungi with their egg-shaped spore packets

Spreading the Wealth

The spores of fruiting bodies are spread by breezes, rain, and even animals. Bird's nest fungi, for instance, have fruiting bodies that grow on sticks and twigs. They produce egg-shaped packets of spores in miniature cups that look like nests. When the spores are ripe, a cover splits open on top of the nest. As soon as a drop of water hits the "eggs," they pop out of their nest, and the spores scatter.

The scientist who named Mutinus elegans, *the elegant stinkhorn, must have been joking. Flies and other insects are attracted to the foul stench of this fungus, which is far from elegant.*

Fungi known as stinkhorns rely on insects to carry their spores to new feeding grounds. Their fruiting bodies are covered with a spore-filled greenish slime that smells like rotten meat. Insects, especially flies, catch a whiff of the foul stench and quickly swarm over the growths. Spores stick to the flies' legs, and wherever the insects go, they spread the beginnings of new stinkhorns.

The truffle, a fungus that grows on the roots of certain trees, has a fruiting body that lies hidden in the earth like a potato. As its spores mature, the truffle gives off a strong scent that lures squirrels and other hungry forest animals to its hiding place. When a creature finds and eats the truffle, the spores enter its stomach, are later released in the animal's dung, and begin growing into new feeding bodies.

Some fruiting bodies can produce enormous numbers of spores. Giant puffballs, which can grow to be as large as sheep, send up clouds of brown smoke containing as many as five trillion

Truffle Hunters

Entrepreneurs on the West Coast do $5–10 million in business each year by selling prized fungi, such as white truffles and morels, to gourmet grocery stores and restaurants. In Europe, where truffles grow abundantly, people use specially trained pigs and dogs to hunt for the prized fruiting bodies.

A western lawn puffball releases a cloud containing trillions of mature spores.

spores. The fruiting bodies of some wood rot fungi have been estimated to give off 350,000 spores per second for as long as six months.

If every spore from every fruiting body found food and began growing, the Earth and everything on it would soon be overrun with fungi. Fortunately, relatively few spores find what they need to live and grow. That is why fungi produce so many spores.

A Taste for Sweets

Human ancestors learned to mix flour, water, and a little honey and leave the mixture in warm open air until it mysteriously doubled in size. When the dough was baked in an oven, it became a soft, light loaf of bread. What these bakers did not realize was that wild yeast, a type of fungus, had invaded the dough and performed a little magic.

Yeasts are microscopic round or egg-shaped cells that spend their time floating through air, hiding in soil and saltwater, or living on leaves, flowers, and animals. Thousands of yeast cells live on human skin and in our mouths and stomachs, and most

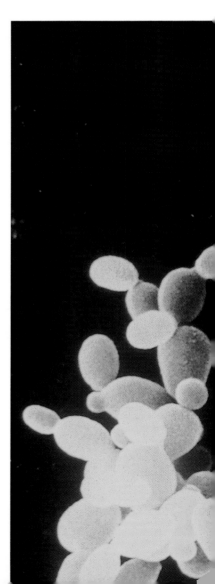

are harmless. There are hundreds of known species of yeasts, and scientists suspect that hundreds of unknowns are hiding around us.

Yeasts belonging to the genus *Saccharomyces* ("sugar fungus") play the biggest role in our everyday lives. When these yeasts land on flour and water mixed with a little honey or sugar, their enzymes work on the sugar to produce carbon dioxide. The gas forms bubbles within the dough, which

Yeast cells in the process of budding (magnified nineteen thousand times)

As yeast cells react with sugars to produce carbon dioxide, the balloon fills up with gas.

expands to double or triple its original size. When given ample sugar but little oxygen, the enzymes change sugar to carbon dioxide and alcohol. Fungi can turn grape juice into wine, grains into beer, apples into hard cider, and rice into a Japanese drink called *sake*.

Yeasts are unique in the way they reproduce. The wall of each cell swells until a second cell, known as a bud, forms. This bud is almost as big as its parent, and in time, it breaks off and begins making buds of its own. Sometimes buds appear on the new cell even before it separates from its parent, and it quickly becomes a chain of buds. As long as its food supply lasts, the chain continues growing. It might eventually consist of more than ten million cells.

Early in the twentieth century, scientists discovered that yeast cells contain high amounts of essential B vitamins, minerals, and proteins. Today various forms of yeast are grown, dried, and sold as nutritional supplements. As we learn more about them, fungi with a taste for sweets might play an even larger role in our lives.

Late blight of potato, a disease caused by the fungus Phytophthora infestans, destroyed about one-third of Ireland's potato crop in 1843.

Chapter Three

Snacking in Fields and Forests

When they first came to the New World, Spanish explorers were introduced to many new and strange foods. One particular plant impressed them with its high productivity and short growing season: the potato. Explorers carried several tubers back home to try growing them on their own soil. By the late 1700s, many Europeans were growing the potato as a main crop. In Ireland, a typical family of six ate about 250 pounds (110 kilograms) of potatoes in a week—and little else. This dependence on one crop was soon to turn into a disaster.

On a spring day in 1843, an Irish farmer noticed that the leaves and stems of some of his potato plants were shriveling and turning brown. When he checked the underground tubers, he found that they were black and mushy. Later he discovered that his neighbors' crops were also being destroyed.

No one knew what to do to stop the disease, known as the late blight of potato. By the end of the year, about one-third of Ireland's crop was lost. Two years later, the organism attacked hundreds of fields. With no way to control it, about a million people died of starvation, and another million were forced to leave their homeland. Not until 1861 did Anton deBary, a German botanist, identify the plant destroyer as *Botrytis infestans*. Today we know it as *Phytophthora infestans*.

Hitchhikers

In the early twentieth century, a fungus called *Ophiostoma ulmi* was accidentally imported to Europe from Asia. It soon began feeding on elm trees in the Netherlands. Once inside the trees, the spores sent out mycelia that spread quickly. The fungus grew into the tissue of the trees and strangled them so that they could not get water or nourishment. Leaves turned yellow, and branches died.

To make matters worse, beetles laid their eggs under the bark. When the larvae hatched, they picked up some of the sticky spores and spread them as they moved from tree to tree. Before long, Dutch elm disease was destroying trees across Europe and North America.

Fungi have left their mark on almost every kind of plant around the world. One mold almost wiped out the grape crops in France; another has nearly destroyed the sweet chestnuts in North America; and still another killed millions of avocado trees in Southern California. Blight molds have attacked pineapples, strawberries, tomatoes, apples, oranges, and many other plants and caused millions of dollars in damage.

More than three hundred species of fungi, known as rusts, attack cereal grains such as wheat, barley, corn, rye, and oats. Rusts cover leaves and stems with ugly reddish-brown spots and eventually kill the plants. Other fungi, called smuts, affect grasses, wheat, and

A deadly fungus called black rust covers stems of bearded wheat with ugly reddish-brown spots.

29

Prized Smuts

Cuitlacoche (also spelled *huitlacoche*), corn that has been invaded by smuts, is a delicacy in parts of Mexico. Because *cuitlacoche* brings a higher price than healthy corn, farmers sometimes deliberately infect their crops with the fungus.

corn. When they land on wheat flowers, the seeds stop growing, and the entire plant starts to smell like rotten fish. Smuts that land on corn produce a clump of gray, shiny, tumorlike growths that look like overgrown kernels.

Poisons

Some fungi have a habit of producing **toxins**, or poisons, that keep small creatures from eating their food supply. While this helps the fungi, it can spell trouble for humans who unknowingly eat the fungus. One evening in 1951, in a small village in southern France, people were awakened by loud screams in the neighborhood. Some villagers were suffering from a strange, violent illness. One man, thinking he was a plane, jumped out of his second-floor window. A woman, trying desperately to escape imaginary flames, leapt from her third-floor room. Five other men, victims of an unknown attacker, fell dead in the street.

The tragedies had everyone stumped. The only thing all of the victims had in common was that they had eaten bread from the local bakery. Although the mystery surrounding their deaths was never solved, the suspect was a fungus, *Claviceps purpurea*.

Today scientists know that *Claviceps purpurea* lives on grasses and cereals such as rye, barley, and oats. The fungus produces small, hard, spur-shaped structures called **ergots**, which are highly poisonous. If ergots become mixed with any

Ergots look relatively harmless, but one of these hard structures can contaminate an entire batch of grains. Here, ergots grow on a rye plant.

Poisonous Fruiting Bodies

Many mushrooms growing in the wild are delicious to eat. Others are extremely poisonous, and eating them can cause illness or even death. Some of the deadly mushrooms look very similar to those that are safe to eat. For this reason, no one should eat wild mushrooms unless an expert first examines them. The fly agaric mushroom, shown at right, is highly poisonous and can be fatal to humans.

grains during harvest, they contaminate the whole batch. Anyone eating the infected grains can develop a disease known as ergotism, to which young people are especially vulnerable.

In 1960, another fungus caused a mysterious disease in thousands of young turkeys in England. The birds either died or suffered severe liver damage. Pheasants, ducklings, calves, and pigs in different parts of the country eventually became ill with the same symptoms.

After some clever detective work, scientists discovered that the animals had eaten feed containing one common ingredient: peanuts that had been invaded by a fungus, *Aspergillus flavus*. The fungus was producing **aflatoxin**, a poison. Farmers began to take immediate action to keep the poison out of products meant for humans.

The disaster in England forever changed the way food items were grown, harvested, and manufactured. Seeds are now stored carefully so that fungi cannot hide in them. Farmers plant crops in ways that reduce the threat of fungi in their fields. Government agencies inspect food for aflatoxins and other fungal poisons. With these safety measures, fungi have become less threatening to humans and other animals.

When brushed up by a rake, spores can cause lung infections and asthmatic reactions. This is a rare and curable occurrence, however.

Chapter Four

Dining on Creatures

One Saturday, a group of teenagers in a small Midwestern town volunteered to clean a neighborhood park. They raked leaves, picked up litter, and painted swings and slides. A few days later, one of the boys became ill with a fever and cough. For a week everyone thought he just had a cold, but when his condition did not improve by the end of the second week, he went to see his family doctor.

The doctor explained that, while raking the leaves, the boy had probably

Shaken Spores

In 1994, more than two hundred cases of an infection were blamed on the dust and spores raised by an earthquake in Northridge, California.

inhaled spores of a fungus, which was now feeding inside his lungs. With proper treatment, the infection was cured. Since this happens only rarely, it should not keep anyone from volunteering to work outside.

A Taste for Humans

Spores regularly cause a variety of lung infections and trigger asthmatic reactions in people. These reactions often become more noticeable after a rainy season or when winds are strong. Activities such as farming, road building, and construction—anything that loosens soil—help spread spores that cause illness.

When people travel, especially to the tropical areas where fungi thrive, they unknowingly pick up foreign hitchhikers. One such invader, *Trichophyton rubrum*, arrived in the United States at the beginning of the twentieth century after settling on the toes of its host. From there it spread to other parts of

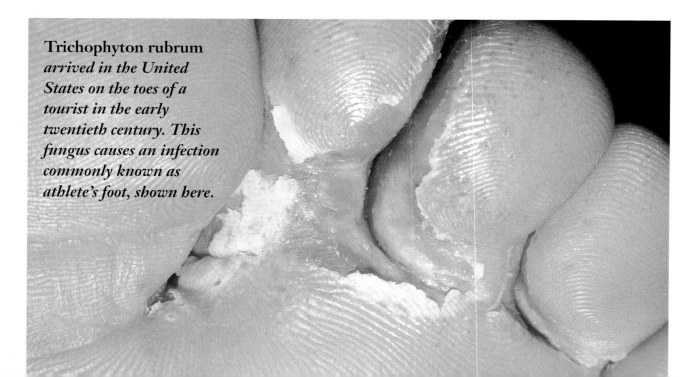

Trichophyton rubrum *arrived in the United States on the toes of a tourist in the early twentieth century. This fungus causes an infection commonly known as athlete's foot, shown here.*

the person's foot and, eventually, to other unsuspecting people. The infection caused by this fungus is called athlete's foot.

Trichophyton schoenleinii, a relative of *Trichophyton rubrum*, feeds on skin, particularly on the scalp. Spread when people share combs, brushes, or hats, this fungus leaves red, ring-shaped circles wherever it goes. People once thought worms were responsible for the infection, so they called it ringworm.

A Variety of Meals

Fortunately, a growing list of drugs helps make fungi less threatening to humans than they once were. The invisible pests still find other creatures to feast on, however. Mice, rats, and squirrels often search for food in warm compost heaps where fungi hide. If the animals inhale the wrong spores, they are doomed. Large numbers of frogs in the rain forests of Australia and Central America have fallen prey to fungi. Toads in the Colorado Rocky Mountains have also been victims.

Fish and their eggs are the favorites of some water-dwelling molds. Water molds attack the fins, scales, or eggs of these creatures and cover them with a white blanket. In time, the floating corpses rise to the surface of the water and slowly disappear as they are digested.

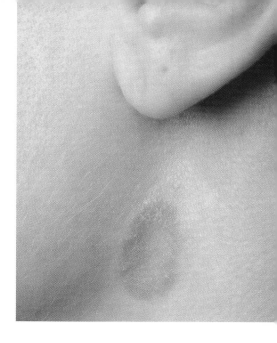

The characteristic mark of ringworm, which is caused by a fungus

Water mold slowly digests a fish.

Small animals, particularly insects, are most vulnerable to killer fungi. Here, a grasshopper serves as fertile ground for a fungus and its fruiting bodies.

The smaller the animal, the more likely it is to be attacked. Insects and other soil dwellers are the most frequent victims. Once spores get inside these organisms, they feed from the inside out.

A microscopic eelworm wriggles closer to a fungus and finds tiny lollipop-shaped knobs sticking out of the end of some threads. These are really traps the fungus has made. The eelworm brushes against one of the knobs and immediately gets stuck. Hyphae begin growing into its body, and within 24 hours, all that is left is the eelworm's skin.

Another soil-dwelling fungus grows hyphae that form loops large enough for an eelworm to slip through. As soon as the worm wriggles through a loop, it is caught in a lasso that tightens while the fungus grows into its prey. The fungus finishes its meal and wastes no time in forming another loop to trap yet another eelworm.

Spores from a fruiting body that resembles a small club land on a caterpillar, and hyphae begin to spread inside the caterpillar's body. After a while, this fungus sends up its own club-shaped fruiting body, commonly called a "vegetable caterpillar." Soon the new "caterpillar" produces spores that will search for other insects to eat.

A fly zigs and zags weakly through the air and lands on a window pane. The insect has been invaded by a fungus that will now slowly feed on it until it dies. Tips of hyphae grow out of the insect's body and fix it firmly on the glass. Soon tiny spores form on the ends of the hyphae, and, when ripe, they scatter around the fly like a halo. When other insects come to investigate the corpse, they pick up some of the deadly specks and soon become fungus food themselves.

Some fungi use chemical warfare to catch their meals. Others have spores in the shape of harpoons that spear tiny creatures. All have unique ways of satisfying their tastes. Silently they wait—and soon after they catch their prey, fungi grow and multiply to begin the hunt all over again.

Tonic

During the 1993 National Games in Beijing, three Chinese women athletes set new world track records. Part of their training involved drinking a tonic made from the vegetable caterpillar.

This fungus-infested creature is barely recognizable as a cricket.

The Indian pipe, a plant whose white leaves and stems cannot produce food, teams up with fungi in a relationship called mycorrhiza.

Chapter Five

Teamwork

One of the strangest plants growing in forests across parts of Canada and the United States is the ghostly Indian pipe, or corpse plant. During the summer its white stems are capped with white, upside-down, cup-shaped flowers. Without green leaves and stems, the plant cannot make food, so a fungus comes to its rescue. When the two meet, the fungus has already teamed up with a green plant and is able to share nutrients from the first plant with its new partner.

Fungi enter into partnerships with many different kinds of organisms. For example, plants supply fungi with the sugars and nutrients they need, and in return, fungi help the plants' roots absorb water and minerals. This plant-fungus relationship is called **mycorrhiza**, which means "fungus root." About 90 percent of plants in nature team up with fungi in this way.

Trees such as sweet chestnuts and apples, as well as plants such as strawberries and tomatoes, produce better crops when they have fungi for partners. The root-dwelling fungus supplies its plant partner with water and keeps away harmful pests. In turn, the plant serves as food for the fungus.

Insect Partners

In the forests of South America, fungi live with millions of leaf-cutting ants in the insects' underground colonies. Each day, worker ants head out to cut pieces of leaves from nearby trees. They bring the greenery back to other workers, who chew it into a pulp and tuck it into their fungi-filled gardens. The fungi go to work on the pulp, breaking it down so that the ants' larvae are able to digest it.

In parts of Asia and Africa, termites build hardened earth nests that are almost 30 feet (9 meters) high. Hidden inside the mounds are gardens filled with fungi that feast on the termites' droppings. The droppings contain debris that the termites are unable to digest until the fungi break it down.

For some reason, the termites never allow these fungi to form fruiting bodies inside their mounds. Instead, when a rainstorm is coming, the termites take bits of the mycelia

Relationships

Sometimes two different organisms form a partnership known as **symbiosis**. This is a relationship in which two dissimilar organisms live closely together so that each one benefits. A relationship in which one organism benefits and the other is harmed is called **parasitism**.

42

This termite hill in Nigeria is about four times the size of the man beside it.

Fungus galleries inside a termite mound

outside and spread them on the ground. Several days after the rain, mushrooms appear and shed their spores. Then the termites gather some of the fungus and carry it to a new mound.

The ambrosia fungus works closely with wood-boring ambrosia beetles. When the female beetle is ready to lay her eggs, she lands on the bark of a tree and begins tunneling inside. As she moves along depositing her eggs on the tunnel walls, she drops spores of the fungus she has carried from her previous home.

The ambrosia fungus feeds on the tree but does not kill it. Slowly it surrounds the eggs like a thin mat, and when the young beetles hatch, the fungus helps them digest the wood. The insects grow and develop into adults, then leave their hideout covered with spores that grow into food for the next generation of ambrosia beetles.

Alga Partner

When a certain green **alga**, or **cyanobacterium**, gets together with a fungus, the two begin sharing and growing as one. This is a lichen, the tiny plantlike growth that often covers rocks. The alga makes food, and the fungus absorbs nutrients from its surroundings. The fungus also protects its partner from drying winds and hot sunlight.

Together, the two organisms are able to survive where few other living things could grow. Lichens live in the blazing heat of deserts and the icy cold of the Arctic. They can even grow

Colorful lichens grow on rocks in Rocky Mountain National Park in Colorado.

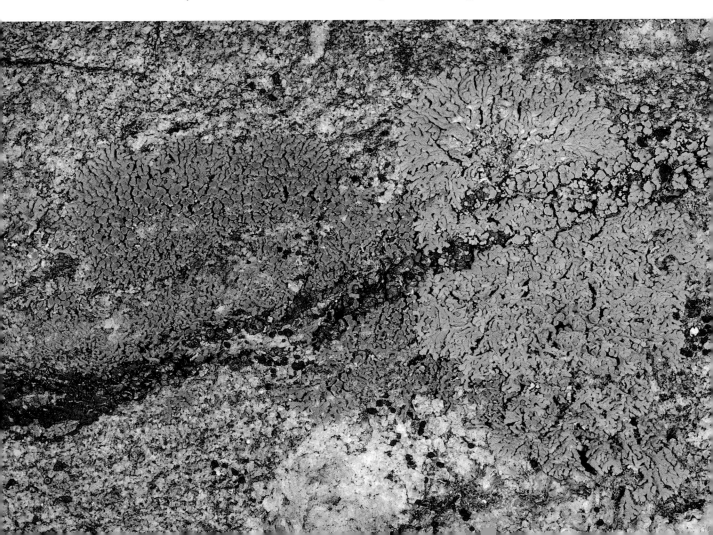

Lichens cover gravestones in Edgartown, Massachusetts.

K-Rations

George Washington's troops are said to have used the liquid from boiled lichens to thicken their soup.

where there is no soil. About 25,000 different kinds of lichens live around the world. They grow not only on rocks, but also on gravestones, abandoned cars, signs, roofs, and the backs of tortoises.

Other living creatures benefit from lichens in many ways. In the Arctic regions, where food is scarce, reindeer lichens make up about 95 percent of the diet of reindeer. Insects, snails, and slugs also depend on lichens for food. Hummingbirds and small mammals line their nests or burrows with them. Villagers in parts of the Middle East turn them into bread. Other peoples have used lichens to make

46

dyes for wool and scents for perfumes and soaps. Litmus paper, a chemical tester, is made from a lichen.

Lichens are also useful in making soil. When they land on bare rock, they give off **acids** that make the surface of the rock slowly crumble. After many years, enough soil forms for plants such as mosses and ferns to grow. Eventually, thanks to lichens, a whole forest might grow where there was once only rock.

Lichens are very sensitive to pollution. Scientists sometimes look for them when testing the quality of air in a certain region. The disappearance of lichens from an area is often a sign that toxic fumes from traffic or factories have invaded the place.

Slow Growth

Most lichens grow at a rate of about 0.5 inch (1 cm) in a year. Some slowpokes grow only 2 inches (5 cm) in a thousand years.

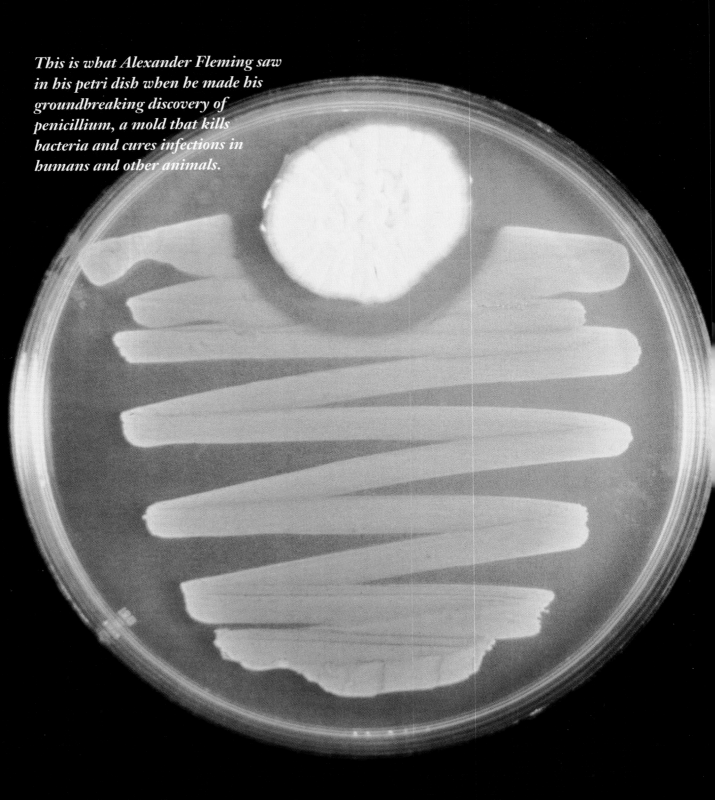

This is what Alexander Fleming saw in his petri dish when he made his groundbreaking discovery of penicillium, a mold that kills bacteria and cures infections in humans and other animals.

Chapter Six

Superstars

In 1928, Alexander Fleming, a Scottish scientist, was studying bacteria in his laboratory in London. One morning, he noticed mold growing in one of his petri dishes. When he examined the mold more closely, he found that the bacteria next to the mold had been destroyed. Fleming later discovered that a poisonous liquid produced by the mold had killed the germs. He wondered if this liquid could also be used to kill germs that attack humans.

Several other scientists, including Howard Florey and Ernst Chain, looked for ways of collecting enough of the liquid to test. In 1941, when a British policeman was hospitalized with blood poisoning, he was treated with the liquid. Within days he improved. His physician had considered the policeman's condition hopeless.

Penicillin, the antibiotic named after the fungus that produced it, was hailed as a powerful new medicine. Not until the end of World War II (1939–45) was enough of it available to treat large numbers of patients. Today chemicals, rather than fungi, are used to make penicillin.

Fleming was not the first to observe the healing potential of fungi. Thousands of years ago, people in Asia treated skin infections with moldy soybeans. Ancient Egyptians rubbed moldy bread on minor cuts and bruises. For a long time, people in China and Japan have valued certain mushrooms, such as shiitake, for their ability to protect against illness. It was not until the early part of the twentieth century that physicians in the western hemisphere began to investigate the sources of these healing powers.

After Fleming's groundbreaking discovery, scientists began searching for other fungi that might produce equally powerful, life-saving drugs. Cyclosporine, made by several different molds, became useful in preventing patients' bodies from rejecting organ transplants. Other fungi have proven helpful in treating heart disease.

Ergots, the hard projections that certain fungi produce on grains, are responsible for a drug that eases the pain of migraine headaches. Beano, the drugstore product that relieves excess stomach gas, owes its existence to a fungus. Yeasts have been useful in many genetic experiments and in studies of the effects of sunlight on living cells.

Fungi have also become superstars in the food and beverage industry. Molds give Roquefort, Gorgonzola, and Danish cheeses their blue streaks and tangy tastes. The citric acid in cola is produced by a fungus. Yeasts play a role in the making of not only bread and beverages, but also such Far Eastern treats as miso, soy sauce, and *ket-jap*, the original ketchup.

Gorgonzola cheese gets its tang and streaky appearance from a mold.

Fungi break down leaves, branches, and other dead organisms in forests, meadows, and fields. As they snack, they release minerals and gases that nourish living plants and animals. They provide food and nesting material for birds and small animals, and they play a vital role in the health of our planet. Thousands of new species of fungi are yet to be discovered. We can only wonder what they will teach us.

Glossary

acid—a sour-tasting chemical compound that turns blue litmus paper red and can combine with metals to form a salt

aflatoxin—a poison, produced by a fungus, that infects crops, especially nuts and grains

alga (plural **algae**)—a simple-celled organism that partners with a fungus to form a lichen

binomial—a two-part scientific name that includes the genus and species of an organism

chitin—a material found in the cell walls of fungi and the outer covering of insects

cyanobacterium—a life form that partners with a fungus to form a lichen

dormant—inactive

enzyme—a protein molecule that triggers chemical reactions, such as those involved in digestion, in living cells

ergot—a small, hard, spur-shaped fungal structure that contains poisons and can infect grains and grasses

fruiting body—a fungal organ that produces spores

fungus (plural **fungi**)—a living organism characterized by a lack of chlorophyll, a cell wall made of chitin, and the production of spores

gills—spore-lined dividers located on the underside of some mushrooms

hypha (plural **hyphae**)—one of many threads that make up the mycelium of a fungus

lichen—a combination of a fungus and a cyanobacterium, growing together as one

mycelium (plural **mycelia**)—the mass of threads that form the feeding body of a fungus

mycologist—a scientist who studies fungi

mycorrhiza (plural **mycorrhizae**)—the relationship between a fungus and the roots of a plant

parasitism—a relationship in which two different organisms live together closely such that one benefits and the other is harmed

phylum (plural **phyla**)—a major category in the classification of an organism

species—a group of closely related organisms

spore—the reproductive cell of a fungus

symbiosis—a relationship in which two different organisms live together closely to the benefit of both

toxins—poisons

To Find Out More

Books

Madgwick, Wendy. *Fungi and Lichens*. Austin, TX: Steck-Vaughn Co., 1995.

Margulis, Lynn. *Diversity of Life: The Five Kingdoms*. Berkeley Heights, NJ: Enslow Publishers, 1992.

Rotter, Charles. *Fungi*. Mankato, MN: Creative Education, 1994.

Silverstein, Alvin. *Fungi*. New York: Twenty-First Century Books, 1996.

Tesar, Jenny. *Our Living World*. Woodbridge, CT: Blackbirch Press, 1994.

Images Online

http://www.wisc.edu/botany/fungi/volkmyco.html
Bold, colorful images of "dead man's fingers," the fungus that attacks houseflies, the fungus that makes ergots, and many others can be found at this Web site.

http://waynesword.palomar.edu/wayne/pljan98.htm
Several different species of lichens are pictured here.

http://www.mykoweb.com
More than eleven hundred photos of fungi are displayed. A CD-ROM version of the images is also available.

Organizations and Online Sites

North American Mycological Association
10 Lynn Brook Place
Charleston, WV 25312
http://namyco.org/
This organization is dedicated to the study of fungi of all kinds.

The University of California, Berkeley
www.ucmp.berkeley.edu
This site gives a detailed look at the various species of fungi.

Mycological Resources on the Internet
http://www.keil.ukans.edu/~fungi/
This site contains a summary of information on fungi on the Web. It has an index and directory for ease in finding topics of interest.

Oregon State University Lichenland
http://mgd.nacse.org/hyperSQL/lichenland/
This site is a detailed yet fun introduction to lichens and their habits.

The University of Michigan Herbarium
http://www.herb.lsa.umich.edu/kidpage/factindx.htm
This site is full of fun facts about fungi.

A Note on Sources

One spring, after several days of rain, the woods around where I live were dotted with mushrooms of every size, shape, and color. Eager to learn more about them, I checked out several guides from the library, including *Mushrooms Demystified*, by David Arora, and *A Field Guide to Mushrooms: North America*, by Roger Tory Peterson. The more I discovered about each variety, the more questions I had. The local librarian recommended a book she thought would be helpful. It was *Introductory Mycology*, by C. J. Alexopoulos.

Several weeks later, I heard about a fungus fair at a nearby college and decided to attend. A variety of mushrooms was on display, and mycologists were present to answer questions. Tables were filled with books and pamphlets; hobbyists demonstrated how to turn mushrooms and lichens into dyes; and gourmet cooks had prepared several delicious treats made with fungi. My interest was sparked even more.

Next I read books such as *Fungal Biology: Understanding the Fungal Lifestyle*, by D. H. Jennings; *The Fifth Kingdom*, by Bryce Kendrick; *Yeasts: Characteristics and Identification*, by J. A. Barnetts; and *Medical Mycology*, by K. J. Kwon-Chung and J. E. Bennett. I also searched for information online, in magazines, and in newspapers to find the material that eventually helped me write this book on fungi.

Special thanks go to two content consultants: Dr. Thomas Volk of the Department of Biology, University of Wisconsin, La-Crosse; and Dr. Kathie T. Hodge, assistant professor of mycology at Cornell University.

Index

Numbers in *italics* indicate illustrations.